GOOSES DON'T HAVE KNEES

BANNING FLYNN

Illustrated by
Atlee Swartz

This little book is dedicated to my grands and my greats with love and endless appreciation for keeping me going!

XOXO
MOO

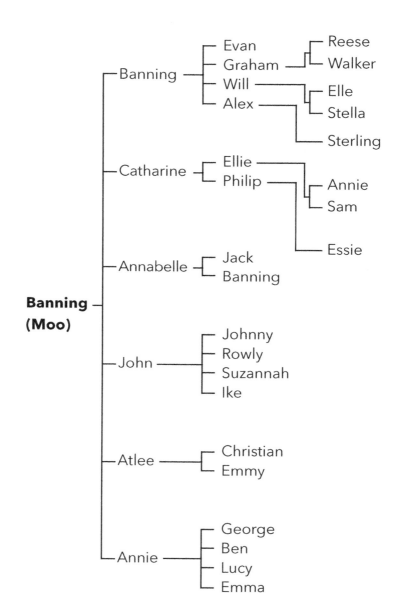

"Out of the mouths of babes oft come gems."
-Unknown

Welcome to the best little book you'll ever enjoy. Years ago, Mr. Art Linkletter proclaimed, "Kids say the darndest things." He was one hundred percent right, but could have gone further! Add to "darndest", funniest, cleverest, most amazingly insightful, kindest, wittiest, and even loveliest.

Enjoy your read.

I know you will!

Part 1

Everything I Know I Learned from my Grands... Well, Almost Everything

If they asked me, I could write a book.

But they didn't.

I wrote it anyway.

Banning at age 2 1/2 , riding in her car seat with
Moo driving, says "Ah-ah-ah-ah. Seat belt!"

So, I buckled up pronto,
corrected by a 2 ½ year old!

Out on Halloween night

Ben at age 3 says, "I don't want any more candy.
I want to go to bed."

Good idea, Ben!

Johnny at age 4 says, out of the blue,
"I don't like to talk about myself."

Oh, how the world would improve
if there were more like Johnny.

Uncle George Stiffler, single and childless, is driving Banning at age 4 to do an errand. In an effort to make conversation, he says, "So, Banning, I see you're rubbing your teddy's tummy, aren't you?"

"Yes, I am and keep your eyes on the road."

What more needs to be said?

Beginning in 2007 (approximately) when Suzannah was 7, she'd insist on a regular basis,
"Moomoo, you've got to get a cell phone.
When are you going to get one? Why not?
You need one. You'd really like it."

Well, for the sake of quieting her (and for no other reason), I gave in. And she was right. I do like it, and all the grands adjust its few signals to their satisfaction!

At Christmas lunch (December 22nd), Aunt Catharine asks everyone at the table to take a turn and say what they're hoping Santa will bring. Emmy, at age 10, says, "Maybe we should take a turn saying what we're hoping to be able to **give."**

Catharine stood corrected!

Moo mentioned something about Atlee's new boyfriend (very new). Suzannah at age 10 ½ says, "Well, how does *Emmy* feel about him?"

Incredibly thoughtful.

Late in May, school ending, Moo says,
"Good work, Christian, for completing 5ᵗʰ grade."

Christian, at 11, says, "It's not good work
unless you've done well."

Correct!

Moo is mixing ½ chocolate and ½ vanilla yogurt
at Menchies. First the chocolate, then the vanilla.
Suzannah at 10 ½ says, "Just pull the middle handle
and it will come out swirled."

(Duh!)

At Starbuck's, Christian, at 11, explains to Moo,
"Tall is the smallest. Then comes Grande.
Then comes Grande Latte."

Thanks for the translation, Christian, and
let me guess which size you want!

Emmy at 11 taught me how to dial into my favorite
tune on the car CD, rather than just waiting until
that particular tune came around.

"You're just too marvelous."

Emmy, almost 12, is helping Moo hang a mirror.
There's no hanger on the back and
Moo wonders out loud, "How the heck
am I going to hang this?"

Emmy says, "Just nail it."

Moo thinks to herself, "Sure, Ems, just blast a nail
or two into it. That should work."

Em explains, "Put two nails for the mirror to rest on
and one bent at the top for security.

Perfect! Thanks, Em!

Emmy at 12 says, "I think it's so cute when
husbands cook supper for their wives!"

It *is* cute, Em!

Moo is commenting on how much she dislikes the new modern phrase, "Love ya" which seems to be said to *everyone*, *anywhere* and *whenever*. Johnny at 14 says, "We need more love in the world."

You're so right.

Love ya.

Moo tells Will her car is a 1991 model.
Will at 14 says, "So, it was made at the time of the fall of the Soviet Union."

(Exactly what I was thinking.)

Moo asked Christian aged 14 ½ what it is that's showing beyond the length of his shorts.
He explained, "Those are called sliders, used to protect your legs sliding into base."

I'd never heard of sliders. Am sure John never wore them. Maybe he never had the opportunity to slide?

Catharine tells Philip age 18 that Moo had pelvic prolapse surgery. Philip says, "I didn't know humans got that. Dad says it's common in cows."

And who but Ron would know?

Mooooooooooooo

Graham in the spring of 20017 (age 24) said,
"Moo we gotta have a family reunion. We've never
really had one, ever!" He pushed and we did
and we will continue for years!

Thanks, Ham.

Evan, 27, warned me to be selective and thoughtful
regarding who I told the sad kitten-saga to.
"Remember, Moo, not everyone has your sadistic
sense of humor. Just be careful."

Amen.

Moo tells Evan that Captain Sullenberger has a definite limp but she's not taking him to the vet yet cause he still eats well. Ev says, "Moo. you still eat even though you have a broken leg!"

Ev, our good doc!

Emma: "You have taught me that I can love a little person from Ethiopia (where?) just as much as I love certain little people from the U.S.A.!"

(Whoever would have 'thunk'?)

Something I learned from Moo is you can't always expect to be put in the book.

-Ikie

P.S. What I hope the grands are learning from me–
the correct use of the words *at* and *good*
and *me* and *I*, etc…!

To be continued…..

Part 2

Out of the Mouths of Babes

Reese, newly potty trained and thrilled with herself, carries her plastic baby potty into Target telling anyone who will listen, "I'm potty trained!"

-age 2ish

Ellie asks Annie who she'd like to say
a prayer for. Annie answers, "GG, Pap, the cows,
and the playdoh downstairs."

-June 2019, age 3 ½

Annie holds Sam in her lap for the first time
and quietly announces, "I don't like him."

-January 8th ish, 2019

Annie, age 3

Sam, newborn

Annie asks Ellie what the yard man is doing in their front yard. Ellie answers, "He's helping." Annie says, "God bless him."

-August 2018, age 2 ½

Ellie and Annie are at a mall. They stop for a snack.
Ellie allows Annie to have three tiny bites of
ice cream. When Annie tastes it she says,
"Moomoo. Yea!"

-January 2018, almost 2

When "GG" put on Annie's new tie-dye sneakers, Annie hopped off GG's lap and started dancing!

-August 2017, 17 months

When the family is at the beach, Annie announces, "We're on 'cation." And then, "Sam, are you ready for 'cation?"

-Great Grands

Annie, age 3

Sam, age 7 mos.

Annie, just about to take a big bite of her sprinkles-covered donut, pauses to say, 'Sam can have one when he grows up."

-Great-Grand Annie, age 3

Sam, 7 mos.

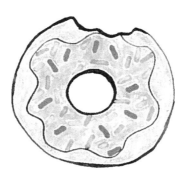

Ike says to his teacher, "Mrs. Jakubisin, I don't have on any underpants!" She replies, "Oh really, Ike." And he says, "I have on boxers!"

-Ike, 3 ½

Ike and Suzannah spend the night with Christian and Emmy. When they return home Ike announces, "Every night should be cousin night!"

-Ike, age 6 ¾

After a close football game in which Ike was clearly the star player, John said, "Ike, you were our Tim Tebow!"

Ike answered, "Dad, I'm not Tim Tebow. I'm Ike Evans."

-Ike, age 11

Ike is pointing at the vase of flowers in the center of the table. Quite an impressive floral display. Moo says, "Wow, just look at those magnificent flowers."

Ike says, "No, is a octopus!"

-Ike, age 2 ½

At 3 am, Ike appears in his parent's room screaming and crying. John wakes up and says, "Ike, are you okay?"

And Ike answers through his tears, "Obviously not!"

-Ike, age 9

Ike and Suzannah are in the bathtub together.
Ike says, "Suzannah, I really love you
but I need some privacy."

-Ike, age 3

Ike is looking at the CD cover of Louis Armstrong.
He asks, "Is he the good bike rider?"
(Mixing up Louis with Lance Armstrong)

-Ike, age 7

Catharine is fingering through Ike's hair trying to feel the scar he claims he has. She can't find it. "Where exactly is it, Ikie?" He answers with a devilish grin, "In my pocket!"

-Ike, age 12

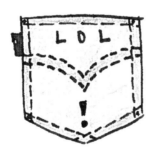

Moo says, totally sarcastically to John, Aly and Ike, "I'll give $100 to the one who guesses what Cousin Quartie said to me when I dropped him off at the Disney Complex. I knew positively they'd never guess correctly. Ike thought for a few seconds, rubbed his chin in thought and said, "Love ya!" Bingo! (They all knew very well how much I detest that expression.)

-Ike, 12 ish

Ike tells his mom his favorite part of the wedding we'd all gone to was "getting to know Moomoo and Aunt Barbara better."

Imagine. Age 15.

P.S. And we liked that best too, Ikie!

Suzannah's pre-school teacher asks each child,
"What makes you happy?"
Suzannah's answer, "Aunt B!"

-age 3

Suzannah and her teacher spot Moo in the hall at school. The teacher says to Suzannah, "Who do I see?"

Suzannah says, "That's Aunt B's mommy!"

Suzannah, walking out of Moo's guest room says, "This is Emmy's room!" (When the Johnsons visited they stay in the guest room.)

-Suz, almost 3

Aly told Suzannah how lucky she was to get to swim with the dolphins in the Bahamas. Suzannah said, 'The dolphins were lucky!"

-age 3 ½

Moo tells Emmy to stop messing with Moo's CDs and to keep them in place. Emmy packs them back up and Suzannah asks, "Did she put the rubber band back on right?"

-age 10 ½

Moo tells Suzannah that she and Aunt Barb are going to a concert, a Cole Porter concert. Suzannah said, "Oh, I sort of wondered 'cause I thought you meant it was a Black Eyed Pea concert."

-Age 10 ½

"Sometimes I think my dad is older than Moomoo."

-Suzannah, age 10

Alex, having never shown any interest in tennis at all, never owned a racquet, swaggers into the kitchen and announces, "Mom, I think I'm gonna be a tennis pro,"

-age 16ish

Aunt B says, "Suzannah, I'm your aunt *and* your Godmother." After much thought and a long silence Suzannah says, "But Aunt B, you can't be a Godmuver. You don't have any wings."

-age 4

Wondering who had opened Moo's Christmas gift basket from the preschool everyone denied the "crime". Suzannah calmly states, "I guess God did it."

-age 7

Suzannah has a brand new pink t-shirt with a raised, rubbery design on the front. Ike touches the design and Suzannah quickly informs him, "Ikie, this is *my* new shirt. Get your own clothes."

-age 4

In 2004 "sister" is commonly used as a term of endearment. Banne (Aunt B) calls Suzannah "sister" and Suzannah puts her hands on her hips and says emphatically, "Aunt B, I am *not* your sister!"

-age 4

After watching a TV program on Siamese twins
Christian asked, "Will I have twins
with heads together?"

-age 8

"Moomoo, did you get divorced from Poppie 'cause
he's for Kerry and you're for Bush?"

-age 8 ½

In 4th grade Christian said, 'Every day there's a new painting in the sky from God."

Moo tells Christian she has two new kittens. Christian says, "That's great Moomoo, now all you need is a computer."

-age 8 ½

Christian asks, "So what's Charlie's new job?"

"He's a salesman at the ABC store" is the answer. Christian then says, "Ya mean he works on television?"

And Atlee gigglingly smirks, "Yeah, any day now we'll see Charlie on Good Morning America!"

--age 11

At Starbucks Christian gives Moomoo a lesson
in Starbucks lingo. Very patiently he explains,
"Moomoo, 'tall' is the smallest, then comes 'grande',
then 'grande latte'."

Thanks Christian for your worldly knowledge!

-almost 11

When a friend asks Christian who people say he looks like, his mom or dad, Christian says, "Harry Potter."

-age 11

Reese calls Walker, her baby brother, "Alkerbaby."
(W is hard to pronounce)

-Summer 2018, age 2 ½

Christian says, "Moo, look at those clouds.
That must be heaven."

-age 13

The heavens declare the glory of God;
the skies proclaim the work of His hands.

Psalm 19:1

Uncle John drives Christian from Florida to camp in Maine. John reports to Moo, "That kid asks 5,000 questions approximately every 3 ½ minutes." So I said, "Christian, you may ask me one more question."

Christian answers, "For how long?"

-age 13

Moo's CD is playing "Younger than Springtime" from South Pacific. Christian comments, dripping with sarcasm and a naughty grin, "Can't get much better music than this!"

-age 11

Atlee, Christian's mom gives him a big hug.
Christian says, "When I have a girlfriend,
can I hug her?'

Atlee says, "Yes, for three seconds."

Christian opens the huge box containing the new unassembled Ping-Pong table, two slabs, 10,000 nuts, bolts, hinges and screws. He comments, "This is not a job for Uncle John."

-age 15

Moo's driving Christian home. He asks to stop at McDonald's. Moo says, "Do you want to get something for anyone else at home?"

Christian answers, "No, I want Emmy to eat only healthy food."

-age 16

Emmy, Christian's sister, asks him if he likes her make-up. His answer, "No, you look better without it!"

Christian is studying his vocabulary words for a test.
When they get to school Moo says,
"Good luck in your test."

Christian says, "Oh I don't care about that.
We have a tough game after."

Christian to Atlee, "Don't worry, Mom.
When I'm older, I'm going to make a lot of money
and I'll take care of you like Evan and
Graham take care of Aunt B."

-age 16

Christian texts from Germany to Atlee,
"Hi mom. How's America?"

-age 16

Christian asks, "Mom, how long do you think Bradley (dog) will live?" Atlee answers, "Probably another year or two."

Christian says, "I hope he lives to see me graduate."

-May 2013, age 17

On Mother's Day, en route home from church, Christian says to Atlee, "Can we stop at CVS so I can get you a card?"

-age 17

Atlee tells Christian, "Moo might move into a tiny cottage on the Evans' property."

Christian says, "Well, I guess there won't be any more great parties there. Is Moo a light sleeper?"

-2013

Christian very seriously tells Atlee that he will be at the upcoming family reunion (2018) but in the future, he may not be able to attend because he'll be working. He hopes the family will understand. We're so proud of you, Christian.

-2017

Moo says, "Guess what I'm getting for the living room. Hint: it starts with PP."

Christian's guess: A port-a-potty

-age 17

When being interviewed by Samford U., Christian
mentions to the representative that he is Alex
Radler''s cousin. The gentleman grins,
"Ah Radler, yep, he used to throw the best parties...
and what a flat screen!"

Emmy to Atlee, "I'm thinking about Moomoo."

Atlee: "What are you thinking?"

"About her drinking chocolate milk."

-age 4

Emmy: "When I get close to the fire
it makes my eyes leak."

-age 4

Emmy whispers in Aunt Banne's ear at the
Interlachen pool, "Thank you for inviting us."

-age 5

Atlee asks Christian what he wants for Christmas.

Reply: "A hug!"

-2018

Evan rides his bike to the hospital to meet his
newborn cousin Christian. He holds Christian's tiny
forearm and says, "It's the same size
as my handlebars."

-Evan, age 14

Emmy touches Moo's necklace and says,
"Nice bracelet."

-age 2 ½

Moo to Emmy, "Guess what Em? The bank up there
on the corner was robbed yesterday."

Emmy replies, "Did they take your money?"

-age 8

Moo gets her meager "art supplies" out and set up on the guest room floor. Emmy beams, "This is heaven!"

-age 8

Moo says to Emmy, "I like your sweater."

Emmy says, "Thank you.
I got it at the Salvation Army."

-age 10

Emmy, Christian and Moo go to the Draft House
for a movie. The food is very expensive and Moo
is $2 short. When we get home, Emmy sneaks a $1
bill into Moo's pocketbook with a note attached
reading, "Love, Emmy."

-age 7

Moo asks Emmy if Mitzi the cat ever jumps into the Christmas tree. "No, she's too mature to do that!"

-age 7

At Christmas lunch Aunt Catharine asks everyone at the table to tell what they're hoping Santa will bring. Emmy says, "Maybe we should say what we're most excited about *giving.*"

-age 10

Over Thanksgiving break Emmy "babysits" for Lucy.
Emmy calls Annie and says,
"Could you please come Aunt Annie and get Lucy?
She won't stop talking!"

-age 11

As Emmy's getting out of the car at school she says, "Oh my gosh Moomoo, I just realized you're dressed like a normal person. No nightie."

-age 12

Moo asks Emmy to look under the guest room bed and remind her what she has stored under there. (Moo's not allowed to bend after surgery.) Emmy looks and says, "Dust."

-age 11

"Moomoo, you have really long ears."

-age 12

Emmy says, "I think it's so cute when husbands cook dinner for their wives."

-age 12

Emmy asks Moo, "Will it be sad when you <u>pass</u>?"

Answer: "No, Em, have a par-tay and play Cole Porter non-stop! Please!!"

-2011

Moo is driving with her arm out the car window. Emmy says, "Moomoo why do you drive like a truck driver?"

-age 13

Emmy to Moo: "Moomoo, don't say anything. I know exactly what you're thinking."

(Uh-oh!!!)

-age 13

Emmy to Moo: "Moomoo, keep your hands on the wheel at position 10 and 2."

-age 13

Emmy to Suzannah: "Moomoo has a key to our house. Sometimes she comes over like a janitor."

Emmy to Moo: "Moomoo, touching the furry hair on your neck is just like patting a dog's hair, backwards!"

(Oh Em, stop, you always say the sweetest things to me!!)

Moo to Em at the 7/11:
"Oh Em, I've got to have that flower pot!"

"Moomoo, no. I don't think it's for sale and anyway,
you have enough flower pots."

(How right you are, Em!)

Emmy asks, "Moomoo, what nationality would you
be if you could choose?"

Moo: "Hungarian, how about you?"

"I'd be black and my name would be
Lucretia Brown."

Moo tells Emmy that Banning's horse, Joey, is very sick and has to be given 16 pills daily. Em glances at Moo's pill container and says, "Well, I guess Joey's right up there with you."

Emmy calls Moo when she returns home from her mission trip and says excitedly, "Moomoo, I just gotta tell you about the wild monkeys!"

-2016

Moo to Banning: "Did you dream about kittens?'

"No, dream about Charlie." (her step-grandpa)

6 a.m. Banning calls from her crib, "Moomoo, I need my checkbook."

-age 2 ½

Banning comes bouncing home after her morning at Chapel Cherubs, her pre-school, singing the "new song" titled, "I Like Myself" and thumps her tiny thumb on her chest with glee!

-age 3

Brother Jack is watching a video on outer space and says he's going into space with his friend, and baby Banning says, "I'm going into space with Moomoo!"

-age 2

Moomoo doesn't fasten her car seat belt and Banning, strapped into her car seat so thoroughly one might think she really *is* going into space, chirps to Moo, "Ah ah ah ah, seeeeatbelt!"

-age 2

Moo to Banning: "Do you want a lollipop?"

"No, too messy!"

At the Radlers for a family lunch party,
Banning walks up to cousin Johnny and beams,
"Hi, I'm Banning and I'm 2."

Johnny answers, "Hi, I'm Johnny. I'm 2 ½ ."

Banning points at Moo's cheek and asks,
"Why's that *crack* there?"

(It's a wrinkle baby Banning!)

-age 3

Banning, talking to Aunt Banne
(her mom's older sister) on the phone:
"Aunt Banne, do you know Moo?"

-age 4

Banning wraps up an Idaho potato in a blanket and
calls it her baby. Moo asks if it's a boy or a girl.

Answer: "It's a boy.
Don't you know potatoes are boys?"

-age 3

Banning asks her mom,
"Do you like being a mother?"

"Yes, do you want to be a mother?"

Banning: "Yes, but what I really want to be is
a tightrope walker."

-age 4

Uncle George drives Banning to do an errand.
Hunting for something to say to this little 4-year-old
niece, he comes up with, "I see you're rubbing your
teddy bear's tummy, aren't you?"

"Yes, I am and keep your eyes on the road!"

Moo asks Charlie if she can get him some orange juice for breakfast. He sing-songs his answer.
"I get along without you very well."

Later Banning asks Moo if that hurt her feelings.
"Oh no no no, Banning. Charlie was just teasing. He always teases, teases, teases!"

And Banning says, "Does he keep all those teases in his fat tummy?"

Moo asks Banning exactly what her duties will be as vice president of her 9th grade class.

Answer: "I oversee the sales of Bojangles chicken for lunches."

Banning wears her new wedge shoes to school. They aren't broken in and she finds them hard to walk in. The Head of Middle School sees her limping and asks if she's all right. She explains the situation and the Head comments, "Well, it looks like your right leg is doing better than your left."

-age 14

Banning tutored brother Jack his senior year at U.Va. in Calculus so he was able to graduate!

-2016

Moo asks Banning why her mom is going to D.C. with her dad on business. Banning says, "Oh Moomoo, they've just become inseparable!"

-2017

Moomoo yawns and Jack asks, "You sweepy, Moomoo?"

-age 3

Jack hears the song, "When a Man Loves a Woman", and asks Annabelle all about it. She tells him someday he will find a beautiful lady and love her and want to marry her and Jack says, "You mean like Moomoo?"

Moo: "Love ya, Jack!"

-age 3 ½

Jack on the phone to Moo calling from Virginia Beach. "We're going away to St. Martin's. Will you miss me?"

-age 4

Jack says, "Great Gran is in heaven
with Princess Diana."

-age 4 ½

Jack, poking at Moo's wrinkled knees:
"I like you even if you're old."

"Moomoo, you're a very good cook."

-almost 5

Jack spills his milk and asks Belle,
"Did Santa see me do that?"

Jack tells Moo, "GI Joe is my very best friend."

Annabelle tells Jack that the Bieschke family may
not be going to camp in July, and Jack says,
"But then they won't get to see me."

-age 5

Moo hands Jack some silly putty during a very long church service. He doesn't want it and says, "Moomoo, this is church!"

-age 6

Jack says to Uncle Marcus, the Pastor, "Why are you going to work? It's Sunday."

-age 9

Jack's message on Moo's phone after her visit to Virginia Beach: "Hello, Moomoo. This is your grandson. You've cleaned everything up at our house and we can't find the chives. Where did you put them? Call us back before 7:30 p.m., otherwise it's too late."

-age 9

Aunt Annie says to Jack, "I wish you were coming to Ethiopia with us."

Jack says, "I would like to, but I might be an inconvenience to you."

-age 15

Jack Stiffler is elected Head of School,
Norfolk Academy, for his senior year.

-2011-2012

Jack answers the phone and takes a message for
Belle. After Jack and I have talked, I ask him what
the message for Belle was. Jack, fresh from exams
at U.Va. says, "Moo, that's good recall questioning."

Jack sends Moo at postcard from Belgium where he is visiting before starting his new job. Card says, "I hope to see you soon and manage your money!"

11 p.m. and the 2014 Family Reunion is drawing to a close. The waiter removes the portable drink bar.
Jack watches it disappear and says,
"Now I know how the people watching the Titanic sink must have felt."

-January 2014

Annie says, "George, don't climb on the furniture."

George puts his big toe on the edge of the coffee table and says, "Dordie, <u>rest</u> his big toe here?"

-age 2 ½

George is trying his best to get a bean bag cushion into the playpen. Annie asks, "Georgie, what on earth are you doing?"

His answer: "Putting a chicken in the oven."

After being told "no" many times, George finally got close to his birthday cake and stuck his finger in the icing and walked around with icing on the tip of his finger saying, "Hallelujah!"

-age 2

George has a sitter for 24 hours. He wakes at 2 a.m. and the sitter gives him his bottle sitting in the rocking chair. He pauses mid-bottle, looks at her and says, "What's your name?"

-age 2 ½

Annie to George: "George, who's your best friend?"

George: "Moomoo!"

-age 2 ½

Atlee to George: "What class will you be
in this year at school?"

"I'm going to be in the garden class."

-age 5

George: "I'm going to finish Mommy's coffee, then I'll be nocturnal."

-age 5

Annie says, "Pass the ball to me, George."

George says, "You mean you know how to dribble?"

-age 5

"What will Moomoo bring me from Florida?
A jelly fish with chocolate tentacles?"

-age 2 ¾

George spies Marcus cutting the grass and with a
twinkle in his eye says, "Look Mommy, an alien!"

-age 3

Pulling into his driveway after the long trek from
camp in Maine, George exclaims,
"I want to drive some more."

-age 5

Annie asks George why he's all dressed in black
for their family dinner at the restaurant.
"So, I'll blend in with the night."

-age 9

At the 2011 Reunion George asks, "Where are our vests?" (Remembering the Sound of Music performance at the last reunion.)

-age 9

"I bet I know what Moomoo's gonna say when we go to Florida for Christmas...let's go to Denny's."

-age 9

Emma loves the black nurse in the pediatrician's
office. George says, "maybe they're
from the same tribe."

-age 7 ½

Moo sends a surprise package of odds and ends
from Millers Hardware. Paint and paper samples,
keys, lots of stickers, samples of this and that. So,
George says, "Mom, call Moomoo and find out
what this is all about."

-age 8

Listening to the voicemail, George asks Annie, "Who's that?"

"It's Moomoo."

George says, "She sounds so young."

-age 9

Ben to George: "George, George, guess what? We get to wear tuxedos for Ellie's wedding!"

George answers, "Cool. We'll look like spies."

George comes over to Moo during the dancing at
the wedding and says, "I bet you think
the music's too loud."

-age 10

George to Annie, "Mom, why do you say
'Radler boys', they're men"

-age 10

Catharine plans a visit to Chicago. When Marcus comes home from work, George runs to him saying, "Daddy, guess what? Aunt...Aunt...Aunt...somebody's come to visit!"

-age 9

George refers to Moo's new Himalayan kitten as a Macadamia kitten.

-age 9

George's Christmas card to Moo is signed, "Moomoo, I can't wait to see your cats when we visit!"

(Guess I know where I stand.)

-age 9

George to Annie: "Mom, I'm not going to heaven if Moomoo isn't there."

(No comment, Georgie.)

-age 10

When visiting George says,
"Moomoo I like your toilet paper."

(I aim to please, George.)

Annie told George Moo would send him to
summer camp. George said, "What a blessing."

"It's so cold here the Democrats are keeping their hands in their own pockets!"

(This kid is unreal.)

-March 2013, age 10

The Bieschkes are visiting Lake Placid and meet a couple of friends at the Grigsbys. After the get together, George says, "Dad has a new man fan."

-2013

Annie to George: "Why don't you come to Honduras with us next year?"

George: "What do you do there?"

"Help the poor children."

George: "I only want to go to the gift shop."

(Hmmm...where do you come from, Mr. George?)

George's main interest in life revolves solely around his hamsters. When Annie tells him Moomoo is all settled in her new old folk's residence, he says, "She's in her natural habitat."

Regarding Moo's new greeting card 'business',
George asks Annie, "Does Moo have
a card factory?"

-2016

George has a pal at school who is from Mexico.
George calls him El Chapo!
-2016

Regarding the ill will and even vandalism toward Moo at her new "habitat", George analyzes the whole situation as anger toward her because she favors Trump. He is 100% right. Amazing insight and wisdom from a 16-year-old.

Annie asks George what he needs for supplies at the start of school. "Oh, I dunno. A pencil."

-age 15

Annie's holding little Lucy and tells Ben she can't hold him, too. Ben says, "Will you be able to hold us both when you get bigger?"

-age 3

Ben was washing the car and Annie was sweeping the front path. Ben says, "That's called teamwork. Mom, you sweep and I wash."

(Oh, that Annie, always cleaning, cleaning, cleaning.)

-age 3

Ben got a bruise on his hip. He asked Annie if she were going to cut it off with a knife. "No, Ben, why on earth would I do that?" George piped up from the other room and called, "'Cause that's what you do to a banana."

-George, age 5

Ben asks Annie: "Mommy, which one is bigger, a great white, Jesus or a King Cobra?"

-age 3

Noticing the ironing board for the first time, Ben asks, "Mommy, is that Daddy's surfboard?"

-age 3

Ben to Annie: "Mommy, what are you going to be when you grow up?"

(What was your answer, Annie?)

-age 3

Again, Ben asks Annie what she's going to be when she grows up, Annie says, "What do you think I should be?"

Ben says, "A princess."

-age 3

Lucy's favorite TV show, "Wo Wow Wuzby" comes on TV. Ben says, "Mom, get Lucy up from her nap. I don't want her to miss this."

-age 3

Annie says, "Come here, Ben. You can sleep
in this nest I made for you."

"Mommy, I'm not a bird."

-age 2 ½

Moo says to Ben dressed in his cowboy boots and
straw hat: "Hi, Cowboy Ben."

His answer in a flash: "Hi Partner."

-age 3

Ben, trying to get Annie to hurry up:
"Come on, you rascal."

-age 3

Out on Halloween night Ben says, "I don't want any more candy. I want to go to bed."

(Whose son are you? Certainly not Jerry Seinfeld's!)

Ben asks Annie: "Is Moomoo the oldest person you know?"

-age 6

Ben asked Annie why Moo gave her her old Volvo. Annie said, "Because she's generous."

Ben says, "Yah, she gave me her jitterbug case."

-age 6

Annie asks Ben what he's going to give up for Lent. The Pastor's son answers, "My Bible."

-age 6

"I know why Moomoo sent me that picture 'cause she knows I like cars and my name's Ben like Mercedes Benz."

-age 6

Ben to George: "What are you doing?"

"Playing with my tongue."

Ben: "Just like a lizard."

-age 4

When asked what his very favorite part of their visit to Virginia Beach was, Ben answered in a split second, "That Aunt Annabelle cuts up my banana."

-age 4

Annie tells Ben he's on thin ice for his behavior.
He quietly asks, "Is it black ice?"

-age 4

Annie tells Ben they're getting Emma from Ethiopia.
Ben says, "Where did we get Lucy?"

-age 4

Ben to George out of the blue: "George, you have buck teeth and lady legs."

-age 7

Ben to his friend: "I have an uncle who's a cat–Captain Sullenberger."

(Name of Moo's cat)

Ben, winning the spelling bee at school decides he doesn't want to go to regionals to compete, so he purposefully misspells his next word, becomes runner-up and gets sent anyway.

On moving day in Crystal Lake, George is helping like a professional mover. Ben is sitting on a chair out front eating popcorn!

-2016

Dropping the boys off at school, Annie says, "Bye my little angels from heaven!"

And Ben says, "Would you say bye my little devils from hell if we were bad boys?"

-age 6

"Does Aunt Bannie live in a mansion?"

"Why do you ask that, Ben?"

"'Cause she has B's on her towels and her dog wears diapers."

-age 7

Lucy leans way over to reach the last piece of apple on the plate. Once she got it she beams, "I gotcha!"

-age 2 ½

Lucy whispers to the cat, "Kitty, you my best friend in whole world."

-age 2 ½

Lucy to Annie: "Mommy, you're the best Mommy in the whole wide world."

Annie says, "Thank you, Lucy."

Lucy says, "Mommy, what does that mean?"

-age 4

Lucy whispers to Annie, "Mommy, tell Duke not to chew my Barbie."

"Okay, Lucy, but why are we whispering?"

"Because I don't want to hurt his dog feelings."

-age 4

Moo calls Annie to ask if it's best to keep bananas in the ice box. Ben asks what Moo called for. Annie tells him and he says, "Hasn't she ever had a banana before?"

-2017

Annie and Lucy are "home alone". Lucy, unprompted, sets the table, wine glasses included, and the two of them play "dinner music" they each knew from their grandmothers, Gran and Moo!

-2019

Lucy comes downstairs to see the bare spot where the Christmas tree used to be and says, "Uh-oh."

-Age 16 mos.

Lucy to Annie: "Remember that time Moomoo made sandwiches? They were the best best ever!"

-age 4

Lucy says in an irritated voice,
"Why don't *I* get a stepmother?"

-age 4

Marcus comes into Moo's condo with all the
luggage and Lucy says, "Remember Daddy,
no running."

-almost 5

After spring break in Florida, Annie asks Lucy,
"Who's your favorite cousin?"

Answer: "Louie" (Banne's dog)

Lucy asks Annie why she's crying.
"Because I'm sad about Charlie."

Lucy says, "Ah geez, you're gonna see him again
in heaven."

-age 4

Lucy's turn to say grace at supper. She closes with "and God bless Moomoo for the pears." (from Harry & David Co.)

-age 4

Talking about the "talent show" at the August Family Reunion, Lucy asks, "Can I be the statue?"

-age 4

Lucy's new personal word she uses for emphasis (in place of darn) is "screech".

Example: "I don't want to wear these screech shoes!"

-age 4

Lucy loves her ice-skating lessons and does very well. Annie asks her if she'd like to be in the upcoming ice show. "Yes, as long as no one's watching me."

-age 6

Annie to a friend: "My mom doesn't cook."

Lucy pipes up, "Yes she does.
She makes turkey sandwiches."

-2013

Lucy writes with chalk on the driveway: "I love Jesus
no matr wut eevin if I am bad. Love Lucy"

-2013

Annie: "How did you do on the spelling test?"

Lucy: "I got 3 wrong. Who cares if it's a C or a K?"

-2013

Lucy gives Annie's friend a birthday present which is her own savings account amounting to $3.64 and writes on the card, "Happy Birthday, Mrs. K. This is all I have. Please share it with Mr. K."

-2013

Regarding Moo's "card business" Lucy asks, "Does she sell from a stand on the side of the road?"

-2016

Annie tells the girls they'll probably sleep in Moo's living room on quilts. Lucy gives that idea some thought and says, "So, it looks like it'll be Emma, me, Moo, and Frank Sinatra!"

-age 10

Emma's been in her crib for naptime since 12:30 pm. It's now 4:30 pm and Annie, the ever-vigilant mama, decides to check on her. Emma looks up and says, "I'm just readin'."

-age 2 ½

Emma seems pensive and Annie asks her what she's thinking about. "Oh, just thinking about God."

-age 3

Marcus is on his way out for a run. Emma looks at him and says, "Daddy, you look incredible!"

-age 3

Lucy says, 'Daddy is like Santa. He's hardly ever home but when he comes, he's fun!"

-2017

Lucy to Annie: "Mommy, are we lower class?"

"No, Lucy, why would you ask?"

"'Cause we're always last to get on the plane!"

Emma's singing in her crib. Annie comes in and asks her if she's singing to an angel. Emma says, "No, mommy's the angel."

-age 2

Annie's dressed for church and Emma says, "Oh Mommy, you look so pretty. You look like Moomoo."

-age 2 ½

Emma's friend says
"My grandma has a TV in her basement."

Emma says,
"Well Moo has bunk beds for each one of us."

-age 4

Annie to Emma, "Oh Emma, you are so sweet. Where did you come from?"

"Oh mommy, you know you got me in Africa."

-age 4

Moo says to Emma, "Emma you have the most beautiful skin. May I have it?"

"No, I need it."

Emma says to Annie at Ellie's bridal shower:
"Mommy, why does Moomoo have
on her nightgown?"

-age 3

Annie asks Emma what she's doing. Emma, age 3,
answers, "Organizing my little cars."

Annie asks Emma to get Moomoo's yardstick.
Emma brings in a stick she found in the yard!

-age 3

Marcus' mother dies and Emma says, "Mommy now
you'll have to share Moomoo with Daddy."

-age 4

Annie tells Emma we're going to call Graham's son,
"Hershey" because his sister's name is Reese
(as in peanut butter cup). Emma says,
"then they'll be s'mores 'cause there's graham
crackers and Hershey and peanut butter.
But we need marshmallows!"

(What a mind!)

-age 8 ½

When Emma heard that Uncle John would be on
TV watching the governor's debate, she said,
"Now I know we're going to be famous!"

-2018

Christian's teacher asks each child what he or she is thankful for. Christian's answer: "Chocolate!"

-age 3 ½

"My teacher has a big dress and a big bootie!"

-age 3 ½

Moomoo is getting into bed and Christian says,
"I've never seen your toes at night. They look like
wizard toes. They're wrinkled."

-age 5 ½

Christian was making a list of Moo's grandchildren
and came up with a total of 17,
this included his dog, Bradley!

-age 6 ½

Christian goes down the water slide for the time
alone and tells Atlee that on the way down he sang,
"Jesus Loves Me" and then said,
"God helped me do it."

Christian's teacher at preschool tells the class
she'll be going to see her children over vacation.
Christian says, "But we're your children."

-age 3

"When I fly in the plane in the air
will I need my floaties?"

-age 3

Christian to Uncle John at the Radlers for lunch,
"Who are you?"

-age 3

Christian winds string all around his feet and ankles
and says, "These are my flip flops
just like Moomoo!"

-age 2 ½

"Where's that big old Charlie?"

-age 3 after Charlie left Oxford

En route to Disney, Christian asks,
"When will we be in heaven?"

(Someone had said to him,
"This trip will be just heaven.")

-age 3

Rowly comes back from a visit to Sarasota and tells
Moo, "Moomoo, I met a man for you. He's 60,
a billionaire from Saudi Arabia."

(I'm waiting, Row. I'm waiting.)

-2012, age 14

Rowly's thank you message for a newspaper article about his Uncle Rowly:

"Dear Moomoo, thank you so much for the article for my birthday. It's nice to know my heritage. Thank you for the $10. Can't wait 'til I'm 1000 and get that $ from you!"

-age 10

Rowly to Moo on her birthday:
"Moomoo you don't act 75."

-age 14 ¾

John says to Rowly, "What's going on with Ike? He must have thrown his brain over the fence. I'll go get a big box to put it in."

Rowly, with a twinkle in his eye says, "No. Get a little box."

-age 6

Rowly to Moomoo: "Moomoo you look like a Chinese wrestler!"

(Moo had made a tiny ponytail in the back of her head in hopes of hiding her bald spot.)

-age 7

Easter Day Hunt 2007: Rowly spies Moo's wallet on a shelf and says, "Oh, I found the jackpot."

-age 9

Moo wonders where the best spot is to put the litter box. Ike wisely says, "Put it in the least used room in the house." And Rowly says, "That would be the kitchen."

-age 13

En route to Camp in Maine, Rowly becomes
thoroughly disappointed by the fact that
New Hampshire has absolutely nothing whatsoever
to do with a new hamster.

-age 4

Rowly is very unenthusiastic about his upcoming
basketball game so John tells him he'll get him
a chocolate donut after playing. The game ends
and John says, "You did so well.
You really hustled for the ball."

Rowly says, "I didn't hustle for the ball.
I hustled for the donut."

-age 4 ½

Charlie asks Rowly to hold the door open as
he carries the platter of chicken out to the grill.
Rowly says, If you say please."

-almost 3

The family is seated in church and there has been
a few minutes of complete silence.
Then the air conditioner turns on and Rowly says,
"That must be God."

-age 3

Rowly is on the potty at Moo's house and Moo comes into the bathroom and says, "Do you need any help?"

Rowly answers, "I need some privacy."

-age 4

Moo says to Rowly, "Move your booty back against the soft pillow."

Rowly says, "That's a bathroom word."

-age 4

Johnny, in regard to Rick Berry scoring 29 points
in the basketball game: "No one gets
30 points on Johnny."

-2018

Moo asks Johnny if he has been watching the
Olympics. "Yes, my dad's favorite is the
women's beach volleyball."

-July 2008

"Moomoo, your memory isn't as bad
as everyone says it is."

-Johnny, age 13

Johnny to Aunt Annie: "Moomoo's on the phone
talking to one of her friends from the 1930s!"

-age 15

Johnny calls Moomoo on the phone: "Moomoo,
Mom and Dad are out. There's no food. I'm hungry.
I have no money. Can you help me out?"

-age 16

Moo asks Johnny if he'd like a peanut butter
sandwich for supper. He answers,
"Do you have a steak?"

-age 7 ½

Dad John is in Washington, D.C. for a business function. He is speaking seriously after the meeting with a gentleman wearing a "serious business outfit". Johnny spots them in the crowd and runs up to them whereupon the man smiles and says, "Well, this certainly is little John!" Dad John says, "Yep, that's little me."

Johnny looks at the man straight in his eyes and says, "I've never seen him before."

-age 8

The Youth Minister asks the Sunday School group, individually, what he or she would do with the last cookie left on the plate. Johnny immediately said, "Give it to someone."

The minister said, "Why would you do that?"

"Because it's better to give than to receive."

On the way home, Dad John asks Johnny where he had learned such a fine statement and Johnny answered Cartoon Network.

-age 8

Johnny is spending the weekend at Moo's. He fishes a lot and keeps the fish in the canoe. Moo suggests he put the fish back in the lake and let them be free. When he does, Moo says, "Oh Johnny, those fish are so happy now. You can't even guess how happy they are."

Johnny says, "Are they as happy as you are to have me here for the weekend?"

-age 6 ½

Unable to remember the name of the family camp, Camp Bellevue in Maine, Johnny refers to it as "the condo of logs."

-age 5 ½

Annie, Johnny's teenage aunt, is keeping an eye on
Johnny for a few hours and says,
"Come on, Johnny, let's go in the pool!"

Johnny answers, "I'm not allowed to go in
without an adult."

-age 4 ½

Charlie says to Johnny, "Your great-great-great
Grandfather Isaac didn't have a TV. Johnny asks,
"Did he have time out?"

-age 5

Johnny says to his kindergarten teacher, Mrs. Sykes, "You are the oldest person I know."

-age 5

"Moomoo, how high do you think Osama bin Laden can jump?"

-age 5

Johnny looking at all the activity on the birdfeeder:
"This must be bird heaven."

-age 5 ½

Johnny lifts his leg up on the porch railing while
tossing crackers to the geese below on the lawn.
Moo says, "Johnny, please don't get up on that rail.
It's too dangerous"

Johnny answers, "I'm just showing the gooses
my knees 'cause gooses don't have knees."

-age 4 ½

Johnny asks his uncle, the Pastor,
"Do you only work on Sundays?"

-age 10

Mrs. Curry, Johnny's preschool teacher left the
preschool to take a position at Rollins working
in the science lab studying rodents. Johnny's
explanation of her departure: "Mrs. Curry used to
be my teacher, but now she's teaching rats."

-age 4 ½

Absolutely out of the blue,
"Moomoo, am I filthy rich?"

-Johnny, age 4

"I don't like to talk about myself."

-Johnny, age 4

(Oh, how proud Great Aunt B would be of this
statement! She always told the children not to talk
about themselves, get the other person to talk
about him or herself!)

Johnny at the table for a huge Thanksgiving feast:
"Moomoo, why don't you have any children?"

-2000, age 4

Alex and Philip ("older" cousins) are on the deck
very involved with their BB guns and water pistols.
Johnny asks them out of the blue,
"And what are you thankful for?"

Of course, the big boys don't bother to answer him
so Johnny just says, "Well, I guess probably guns."

-Thanksgiving Day

Johnny says he's going to be in Viv's wedding
"and carry some pillows with diamonds on them!"

-age 3 ½

When the twins came home from the hospital
wrapped in a pink and a blue blanket, Johnny says,
"I want to talk to the pink one."

-age 3 ½

Johnny looking at Moo's desk says, "When I have my new house, I'm going to have a desk where I'll pay the bills."

-age almost 4

Johnny's teacher lost her voice. Johnny says to her, "I don't need to talk. You can have my voice,"

-age 4

Moo says to Johnny, "Don't tickle Annie too much, she'd laugh so, so hard!"

Johnny says, "Like a hyena?"

-age 2 ¾

Johnny tells his dad he wants to catch some lobsters so he can give the to Aunt B and Poppie, Aunt Barbara and PopPop, and Mimi and Moomoo and Aunt Charlie!"

-age 3 /12

Johnny swishes off the sand with his hand from the corner seat of his outdoor sandbox and says, "Sit, Moomoo."

(Imagine the thoughtfulness.)

-almost 2

"Squash's tail is a cable cord."

(Squash was the cat. Johnny's grandpa worked in the cable industry.)

-age 2 ½

After Graham's tennis lesson, he watches Moo and her friends play doubles. When changing sides, he says to Moo, "How old is Mrs. Allen?"

Moo answers, "About 45ish."

Graham says, "She looks 18!"

(How true, but we like her anyway.)

After watching the match for a few minutes, he says with a magnificent half-smile, "Moo, I didn't know you could run!"

-Graham, 14ish

Graham, in the car listening to a story Banne is telling him. When the story ends, Graham exclaims, "Mom, that's fascinatin'!"

-Graham, age 4

The four Radler boys, ages 8,6,4 and 2, with Banne
driving and Moo the passenger, are headed to the
store. On the sidewalk is an enormous St. Bernard.
Banne says, "Look everyone.
Look at that huge dog!"

And Will pipes up from the back of the van,
"Not a dog. Is a cow!"

-Willie, age 4

Evan is riding with Moo to the airport to meet
Annabelle when Atlee runs over to the car and
asks, "Aren't you taking Graham to the airport, too?"

Evan's response, "No Booba's too rambunctious!"

-Evan, age 4

Evan and his dad, Michael, and Moo were poolside, teasing and joking with each other. Finally, Moo said to Evan, "Oh Ev, I'm just going to have to push your Daddy in the pool, and Evan sheepishly looked up at me with his twinkling blue eyes and asked, "'Out his floaties on?"

-Evan, age 3 ½

At the base of Moo's house on Alabama Drive there was a slight irregularity in the wooden foundation. One of the Radler boys spotted it and said, "moomoo, the big bad wolf could come and blow your house down."

Catherine being a voracious reader herself, felt Philip at 4 ½ should be moving along with his reading at a faster rate so takes him to tutoring regularly. Upon his return home after a tutoring session, Phil spies his best friend and neighbor, a 90-year-old retired, respected physician. "Woody" was in the yard and Phil hops up to him and asks, "Woody, do you know how to read?"

Made in the USA
Columbia, SC
19 January 2020